EDIBLE?
INCREDIBLE!
PONDLIFE

by

Marjorie Furlong

&

Virginia Pill

Naturegraph Publishers, Inc.

Library of Congress Cataloging in Publication Data

Furlong, Marjorie, 1917-
   Edible? Incredible! Pondlife.

   Bibliography: p.
   Includes index.
   1. Cookery (Wild foods) 2. Plants, Edible—
Identification. 3. Pond flora—Identification.
4. Pond fauna—Identification. I. Pill, Virginia B.,
1922-   joint author. II. Title.
TX823.F87   574.6'1   79-27779
ISBN 0-87961-084-0 Cloth Edition
ISBN 0-87961-083-2 Paper Edition

Naturegraph Publishers, Inc., Happy Camp, CA 96039

For people everywhere who love the pond life

Acknowledgements

To our husbands who have contributed so much by their encouragement, help on innumerable expeditions, advice, and extra hands around the house, allowing us free time to work;

To Jim Tobin for his help with the photography;

To Jim and Marcie Kotula for their help on the wild rice, turtles and leopard frogs; to Steve and Ruby Gray for their help with the turtles and clams; and to many other helpful, enthusiastic nature lovers throughout the United States, we express our gratitude.

CONTENTS

GRASSES & HERBS

TREES & SHRUBS

ANIMALS

RECIPES

INTRODUCTION

During the lengthening spring days, nature prepares one of her innumerable stages, ponds, for an incredible drama. The thousands of pond inhabitants, great and very small, are interdependent actors in each pond's life story. As the days grow warmer the gently pulsating life turns into frenzied activity. The stage is ready for its summer production! By late fall, when the show is about over, some of the actors will migrate; some will go into a well-earned sleep or dormancy; some will have lived complete life cycles, producing seeds for future generations; while others will remain to just subsist on the diminished food supply. Despite the perils facing them, the pond's hardy community of plants and animals will await nature's on-stage call again next spring.

Some 1.5 million natural and man-made ponds are scattered across the United States, with countless more in Canada. Experts find no easy way to distinguish a pond from a lake, or a bog from a pond; but a pond can generally be described as a shallow, rather small body of fresh water with a fairly uniform temperature throughout. No two ponds are alike, even when a short distance apart; nor does one remain the same for very long. Pond life is an endless variety show!

Natural ponds originate from various phenomena. Some form near river deltas when silt deposits dam off parts of the stream; many are caused by erosion and mountain landslides, or by meandering streams in a flat valley; others are glacial ponds, potholes, and kettles. Beavers, nature's master builder and engineer, used to dot the landscape with a great number of ponds before being trapped almost to extinction. Today, man-made ponds outnumber natural ones in the United States. Just a few of the ponds resulting from man's activities may be ditches, reservoirs, stock-watering holes, fish-breeding ponds, quarry ponds, and mill ponds. Often they are built to supply irrigation or to attract waterfowl.

Regardless of how a pond is first formed, a succession of plants soon appears. Certain "pioneer" plants are the stars for awhile, but through their death and decay the soil is enriched with organic nutrients which allow other plants to appear. Thus the pond becomes more and more shallow, due to the accumulating sediment. The opposing shores, where cattails and bulrushes have danced through many seasons, eventually join, until there is no more open water. The pond has ceased to exist. Miraculously, this pond becomes a wet meadow which in time could become part of a forest, and a new natural setting for totally different life dramas. This sequence of events is unpredictable and varies according to latitude and altitude, as well as geological and biological factors. However, a person in his or her lifetime can observe the birth, youth, maturity, old age and death of a pond. Its inhabitants and their descendents move on to act out their life story in fresh new ponds.

From early spring until late fall the pond's food factories are powered, directed and controlled by sunlight. Even in winter, the roots of aquatic plants are storehouses of valuable nutrients. It may seem strange, yet the most important plants in the pond community are not the conspicuous cattails or pond lilies, but the tiny one-celled plants, the phytoplankton. They nourish nearly all the animals large and small, directly or indirectly. Large plants actually support relatively few large animals. Most ponds, however, produce enough to share their edibles with you. The common edibles we describe and illustrate were found in and around ponds located in various regions of the United States. At all stages of pond life, they yielded edibles that were truly incredible!

So why not join the audience and participate in one of nature's greatest outdoor productions? The ticket is free, just be sure you have permission when you visit that nearby pond. The only other requirement is a little time; for very little energy is needed to observe the plant and animal performers. The show starts early, though, and can last all day, so bring your family and friends along for a ponding picnic.

Before You Begin...

Here are five simple hints to guide you in your quest.

1. Of course, make positive identification of a plant or animal before eating. A good rule to follow is to eat only a small portion when first trying any new food.

2. Do not gather and eat anything from a polluted pond or wetland. If in doubt, be safe by soaking and washing plants in a Halazone solution of 5 tablets to 1 qt. water. Halazone can be purchased at any pharmacy. A solution of household bleach (1 tsp. per qt.) may also be used.

3. Observe carefully the quantity of any plant or animal before taking even a small amount. Never take a rare or endangered species.

4. Leave all areas as clean as found, or even cleaner; do not litter.

5. Never trespass on private property. Observe all rules of public lands, and obtain a fishing or hunting license when necessary.

And here's a list of bring-alongs for the well-equipped "ponder." Since you will be going into fresh-water areas, you will be needing some **mosquito repellant**, if you haven't been taking plenty of Vitamin B. In most areas, a small **boat** will be best when fishing; however, **hip boots** will do well for shallow ponds. Your **fishing pole** for hooking that elusive trout can double for catching frogs with artificial flies if you have rejected the idea of using a **spear**. An important item is the **fish net** that may be used for fish, crawdads or frogs. Plastic **buckets** are superior to metal. A **wide-mouthed basket** is best for collecting wild rice. Remember your **knife** for cleaning your catch, and **plastic bags** to keep the meat clean. After you remove your lunch from your **ice chest**, there will be room for your fish. You will need a **shovel** if your quest includes the water lily, wappato or skunk cabbage. **Gloves** and **scissors** are essential for gathering nettles, but would also come in handy for rose hips, mint and Labrador Tea. Bring along plenty of **containers** so that you may keep foods separated. Berries, in particular, should be in several small containers rather than one large one to prevent them from being smashed.

Have fun!

GRASSES & HERBS

Burreed

Sparganium spp.   **Burreed Family**

Burreeds frequently grow with their close relatives, cattails, in fresh-water marshes and along the margins of ponds. About twenty species inhabit the temperate and cool regions of both the Northern and Southern Hemispheres. The burreed pictured, *Sparganium angustifolium*, or Narrow-leaved Burreed, is found throughout the cooler regions of North America, ranging from British Columbia to the San Bernadino Mountains in California.

These herbaceous, aquatic plants are perennial, with creeping rootstalks and fibrous roots. The erect or floating stems and the long, narrow alternate leaves are sheathed in a bulbous base. Mature leaves of burreed vary from ankle-high to shoulder-high, or they sprawl or float. Partly hidden among the leaves are the stems bearing the round, tight clusters of flowers toward their ends. The upper flower clusters, which are male, soon wither; then the female lower flower clusters form hard, burlike balls of seeds.

Edible parts of burreeds are the seeds, the young tender base of stems and leaves, and the rootstalks and tubers. The nutty-tasting seeds provide the hiker with protein for a nutritious snack. Pick mature seed balls when green or brown and dry thoroughly before trying to separate the seeds from the bur. When dry, roll the ball of seeds between the fingers to loosen the seeds. Shake the seeds in a fine sieve to remove the "chaff." Cracked or ground seeds can be used in breads, muffins, or cooked for cereal. Green or dry seeds are a crunchy addition to fruit or vegetable salads.

The succulent lower portions of burreed leaves and stems, and the tender rootstalks and tubers are delicious served raw in salads, or steamed or boiled in a small amount of water, then seasoned with butter, salt, pepper, and a bit of lemon. Also try sautéeing the tender rootstalks, tubers and tender parts of leaves and stems in butter for a few minutes. A good substitute for sedge, burreed may be used in the Stir-Fried Sedge recipe on page 84. (See also recipes on pages 79 and 81.)

Burreed (*Sparganium spp.*)

Warning: Be safe, wash and soak the leaves and roots of burreed in Halazone solution (see page 10) unless absolutely sure the pond or marsh is free from pollution.

Cattail

Typha latifolia (Broad-leafed)   **Cattail Family**
Typha angustifolia (Narrow-leafed)

Native to Central Asia, the ten to twenty species of the genus *Typha*, commonly known as cattail, are now found on several continents and in over half of the United States. This useful wild edible plant can be a problem for farmers when it becomes entrenched in ponds and swamps. Highway department crews find that once established in drainage ditches, cattails can be very difficult to eradicate. But contrary to its reputation as a nuisance, every part of the cattail plant is either edible or useful in some way.

Wash thoroughly the young shoots of cattails and the white stem inside the lower leaves, and then eat like celery or cut into pieces and steam. In early spring you can find the young spikes hidden in a leaflike sheath. Break off the heads and drop into boiling water for 3 to 4 minutes. Remove from water, cover with butter, salt, and eat like an ear of corn. When the spike or head first appears above the leaves, the area above it is loaded with pollen (see picture). Shake off this golden powder and use it mixed with flour in muffins, breads

Young spike of cattail   Cattail roots (*Typha angustifolia*)
(*Typha angustifolia*)

13

or pancakes. This pollen contains protein, fat and vitamins. The root can be gathered and used as a starchy vegetable year-round. Wash thoroughly and peel. The starch can be dug out first or the whole root can be cooked and later strained to get rid of the fibers.

In the fall of the year, snip cattails to add to dried floral arrangements. Other uses for the plant are insulation, ticking, or stuffing—gathered from the cattail heads after they go to seed. The root fibers can be twisted into cord, and the leaves are used for weaving into mats or baskets. Use only the leaves which do not surround the cattail stem for weaving purposes. (See the Cattail Pollen Muffins recipe on page 76.)

LILIES

Scented Pond Lily, Fragrant Water Lily

Nymphaea odorata   **Water Lily Family**

Scented Pond Lily forms massive growths in fresh-water ponds, lakes and waterways. It is widely distributed throughout the United States and parts of Canada.

This perennial aquatic plant is well-known for its especially beautiful and fragrant white flowers. Attached to a long stalk, the flower floats on the surface and opens from about 8 A.M. to 2 P.M. Its large, rounded leaves split to where the long stems attach near the center. Usually lying flat, the leaves also curl up enough to reveal the underlayer of purplish red beneath the smooth, green, upper surface.

The young unopened flower buds of the Scented Pond Lily are most palatable when the stamens are removed and the petals are soaked overnight in soda water. Drain and rinse in fresh water. Boil

Scented Pond Lily (*Nymphaea odorata*)

for a few minutes. Season with butter, salt and pepper. Try cooking the young unfurled leaves for about 8 minutes in salted water. Serve with an oil and vinegar dressing.

Water lilies of all species are often considered weeds because they clog lakes and waterways, causing silting problems and hazards for boaters, swimmers and anglers. However, water lilies, aside from being edible, beautify ponds and lakes, and provide a haven for small fish and other small aquatic animals.

Yellow Pond Lily, Western Yellow Pond Lily

Nuphar advena (Yellow)   **Water Lily Family**
Nuphar polysepalum (Western)

Extensive growth of Yellow Pond Lily is found in fresh-water ponds, lakes and slow streams from Alaska to California, east to the Black Hills of South Dakota, and Colorado. Its many water lily relatives are widespread throughout the world.

A perennial aquatic plant, it is easily recognized by its large, round, smooth, heart-shaped green leaves. These either float or grow

Western Yellow Pond Lily (*Nuphar polysepalum*)

erect on long stalks that are attached to sizable, fleshy, horizontal rootstalks buried in the silty lake or stream bottom. The remarkably large rootstalks are covered with scales (see photo). This species of water lily has a single, waxy, yellow flower with nine sepals surrounding its petals; most water lilies have six.

Yellow Pond Lily seeds are a novel treat to the taste buds after they are dried and popped like corn. The dried seeds can also be ground into meal. Some say that the root is very good boiled for a potherb after parboiling; others say to wrap it in foil, bake in hot coals, dry, and pound into flour. From our personal experience we have found that the root is very bitter after repeated parboiling. Therefore, we can recommend the root only for emergencies.

Western Yellow Pond Lily roots
(*Nuphar polysepalum*)

Mint

Mentha spp.   **Mint Family**

Lemon Mint (*Mentha spp.*)

Widely distributed around the globe, especially in the temperate zone, mint is the common name for a strong-scented herb, a perennial of the genus *Mentha*, which consists of about twenty-five species. We have Lemon Mint in our garden, a cultivated wild plant transplanted from a swampy area, as pictured above. Some species of mint prefer to grow in rich, wet soil near lakes, swamps, ponds, and streams. A pretty, often unnoticed plant, mint will pleasantly scent an entire area on a hot, humid day. To check correct identification, crush a leaf or two to see if the spicy, pungent odor is emitted.

The different species hybridize easily, so identification can be confusing. To mention a few kinds, *M. spicata*, known as spearmint, has smooth leaves and lax, tapering flower spikes. Peppermint, *M. peperita*, can be identified by stalked, smooth leaves and an oblong terminal spike of flowers. For this wild variety, look for soft, hairy, lance-shaped leaves with edges coarsely toothed, arranged opposite on a squared stem. Pale, purplish-pink flower clusters are located at the base of the leaves during the summer months.

Mint is grown commercially for extracts in products such as candies, gum, mouthwashes and toothpastes. Wild species have long been used for flavoring, medicines, jellies and tea. Fresh leaves can be added to green or fruit jello, and to casseroles. (See recipes on pages 76, 79, and 80.)

Nettles, Stinging Nettles, Indian Spinach

Urtica dioica   **Nettle Family**

Nettles thrive in the rich, moist soil around ponds or along creeks and rivers. They are especially abundant in the Pacific Northwest. About thirty species are distributed throughout the world.

Nettles (*Urtica dioica*)

This perennial or annual plant has a single four-sided stem that grows 2 to 8 feet tall. The leaves are coarsely notched, crinkly, dark green, and grow opposite along the stem. All parts of the plant are armed with hollow silicone hairs which, when lightly touched, can cause a painful but not serious sting for hours, even days for some people. During the summer months, several small, greenish flowers cluster in pairs along the stem at the base of the leaves. The plant's spreading rootstalks can cause such prolific growth that nettles are usually considered noxious, unfriendly weeds. Nevertheless, we rate nettles as an edible that really is incredible! The cooked or dried leaves are rich in iron, protein and Vitamin C; and because it grows abundantly year after year, with no human effort, it could be an important source of food in many parts of the world.

The best time to forage for nettles is early in the spring. Of pioneer stock, our families have always eagerly awaited the advent of the first tender shoots, even though not driven by necessity as were our ancestors. In the Pacific Northwest a "mess of nettles" can usually be picked by March. Tender, new plants that are only a few inches high are best. As the plant matures, it gets tough and usually becomes infested with insects. **Caution:** Gather nettles *only* with gloves. Use scissors or a knife to snip off the young plants.

Nettles can be substituted in any recipe calling for spinach. The tender, pink underground stems, which can be pulled up or dug when gathering young shoots, add richness to a pot of greens. European species of nettles are said to produce fine linenlike fiber. The leaves, stems and roots were once used medicinally by western American Indians, and they used the stems for weaving fishing nets and cords. (See page 84, on how to cook, freeze or soufflé nettles.)

Pondweed, Floating Brownleaf, Floating Pondweed

Potamogeton natans   **Pondweed Family**

A member of a large family of aquatic seed plants, Floating Brownleaf or Pondweed is found growing profusely in fresh-water ponds and quiet waters from Alaska and California to Newfoundland, North Carolina, Illinois and New Mexico.

Pondweed (*Potamogeton natans*)

This species of pondweed has brownish-green, rounded, floating leaves that are widest halfway from base to tip. The submerged leaves are narrow and ribbonlike. Spikelike flowers emerge on the surface among the floating leaves, May to July. The seeds are about ⅛ inch long and have a wrinkled, shiny skin. During the summer, pondweeds form floating mats of leaves along with other water plants. They also make dense underwater growth which provides cover for fishes and other small animals.

Pondweeds are perennial plants that, in winter, utilize the food stored during the summer in their rootstalks and tubers buried in the mud. The forager aiming to survive by digging these starchy roots should be prepared to get wet! We like to gather young root stems to nibble raw, and find them slightly nutty tasting. The rootstalks are a nutritious addition to salad or stews.

Reed Grass

Phragmites communis   **Grass Family**

Large clumps of Reed Grass can be found growing in fresh-water swamps and marshes, or around springs. It is widely distributed throughout the temperate regions of the world.

This is one of the few species of grass that likes to have its feet wet. Reed Grass is rather easy to identify by its over-the-head stature and its large plumelike flower clusters. Their summer-blooming flowers are purplish when young, light-colored and fluffy when old. Long, flat leaves loosely encircle a hollow, stiff stem in rows of two. (See Sedges for directions on edible parts.)

Reed Grass (*Phragmites communis*)

Rushes

Juncus spp.   **Rush Family**

Rushes commonly grow in shallow fresh-water and salt marshes throughout much of the world.

These usually perennial grasslike plants vary from knee-high to five feet or more. The stems are hollow or pith-filled, with hollow or flattened leaves. By summer, blooms appear in clusters on or near the tip of the stem. As with sedges, it is difficult to distinguish between the over 200 species of Rushes. (See Sedges for directions on edible parts.)

Rushes (*Juncus spp.*)

Sedges

Carex spp.   **Sedge Family**

Many different species of sedges grow along the edges of inland fresh-water bogs, ponds, lakes, marshes and wet meadows. They are common throughout the world.

Sedges (*Carex spp.*)

Sedges are either annual or perennial grasslike plants. The over 2,000 species are difficult to identify. They grow singly or in clumps, ankle- to shoulder-high. The solid stem can be triangular, quadrangular or flattened, with the base of the leaves growing tightly around the stem in rows of three. Inconspicuous flowers, growing in spikelets from the leaf axils, bloom during the summer.

Among the three plant groups of Reed Grass, Rushes, and Sedges, the edible parts are the roots, the tender young stems and leaves, and the dried seeds. These common, often considered pesky plants, could be eaten for survival. The roots can be boiled, roasted, or eaten raw. In the spring, the tender stems and leaves are delicious and nutritious raw, in salads, or boiled as a potherb. The dried seeds can be made into flour or cooked as cereal. (See recipes on pages 79, 83, and 84.)

Skunk Cabbage, Yellow Arum

Lysichiton americanum   **Arum Family**

The Skunk Cabbage, a respectable plant with an odoriferous name, is found in shady wet areas from Alaska to California on the West Coast, and east to Montana. Other species with the common name of Skunk Cabbage are found across the United States and Canada. As it apparently prefers peat moss, you will often find it growing in bogs along with Labrador Tea and wild cranberries. Also cropping up along the edges of commerical cranberry bogs, the tenacious Skunk Cabbage can be a real pest to the farmer.

Skunk Cabbage (*Lysichiton americanum*)

Skunk Cabbage is a perennial plant with large, oblong leaves which are heavily veined. A large yellow, lilylike flower is embedded in a fleshy spike and appears before the leaves in early spring. The sizable, starchy roots were used by the Indians, who steamed them in underground pits. They also dried the roots for medicinal purposes to cure about twenty different ailments. A liquid made from the boiled roots was used as a contraceptive that could cause permanent sterility.

When the young unfurled leaves come up in the spring, they can be collected and boiled as a potherb. Change the water several times to eliminate any characteristic odor. The roots can be collected, washed well and separated into small bunches so they will dry without molding. When thoroughly dry, grind them into a flour, which has a peppery flavor and is recommended as a survival food only. **NEVER** eat any part of Skunk Cabbage raw, as there are calcium oxalate crystals embedded in all parts of the plant which burn the mouth and throat. These crystals are destroyed by cooking, steaming, lengthy drying, or roasting.

Wapato, Arrowhead, Duck Potato, Wild Potato

Sagittaria latifolia   **Water Plantain Family**

The Wapato, also commonly called Arrowhead, grows in shallow fresh-water ponds, ditches, or slow-moving streams with its roots imbedded in soft mud. Some forty species are scattered throughout the United States, Canada, Asia and Europe. We found the species illustrated flourishing in irrigation ditches in the Sacramento Valley of California, and in eastern Washington. We also saw great clumps of a species of *Sagittaria* along the backwaters of the Mississippi River in Missouri.

This perennial plant has large, distinctively arrowhead-shaped leaves, that either float or emerge above the water, supported by long, fleshy stems. White, three-petaled flowers appear in July or August growing in whorls of three along the stem. These lovely flowers have either pistils or stamens that can occur on separate

Wapato *(Sagittaria latifolia)*

29

plants. By fall the rootstalks have produced edible starchy tubers. These are lavender and brownish colored, and they vary in size from a pea to a hen's egg. Wapato is a persistent plant despite modern methods of ditch digging and cultivation. Also called Tule Potato, it still grows abundantly around the islands of the Sacramento and San Joaquin rivers. There it is cultivated and eaten by the Chinese.

The common name, Duck Potato, reflects the fact that *Sagittaria* is sometimes planted as a food for waterfowl. Indian legends are woven around this plant, which they called "Wapato," and which was an important food for them. When the white man arrived, the tubers became an item of commerce. The journals of Lewis and Clark mention that they purchased the tubers from the Indians during their stay at Fort Clatsop, Oregon, in the winter of 1805-1806. What a welcome treat the tubers must have been after the expedition's usual fare of wild game!

When gathering wapatos in the fall, it is not necessary to destroy the plant to harvest the tubers. Try to dislodge the tubers by digging gently or feeling around in the mud away from the base of the plant. The dislodged tubers will float to the surface. Indian ladies used to break the tubers loose with their toes, which is still a good way. (See the recipe section, pages 81 and 83, for ways to serve these delicious, nutty-tasting tubers.)

Watercress

Nasturtium officinale   **Mustard Family**

A member of the large mustard family, watercress is a well-known salad plant which was introduced long ago into the United States from Eurasia. It is found world-wide and has been enjoyed since ancient times. Watercress and its related species like to grow in masses on stream banks and along edges of ponds.

Watercress (*Nasturtium officinale*)

The stems of cress float, grow erect or lie prostrate on the ground. The roots will grow at the nodes (joints of leaves and stem), attaching when in contact with mud to form a creeping plant. Along the branching stems, the leaves are composed of leaflets with the terminal leaflet the largest. Clusters of tiny white flowers appear in spring and summer near or at the terminals of the plant.

Watercress is rich in both iron and calcium, plus the vitamins A, B, C, E and G. For those who have a juicer and a good supply of watercress, this vegetable makes a healthful drink. Combined with other juices such as tomato or carrot juice, it adds a delightful crispness. Add a little water to the juicer, or follow the recipe listed for spinach or lettuce if watercress is not included in your juicer booklet. You can also use a blender and strain. Cress makes a fine addition to soups or stews.

To cook as a potherb, pour boiling water over leaves and drain. Add water and boil for five minutes and drain again. Add small pieces of crisp bacon and serve with vinegar or hot sauce. Watercress can be enjoyed in a tossed green salad or by itself with your favorite dressing. (Also see recipe on page 82.)

Warning: Watercress will grow in polluted areas, so as a precaution if questionable, soak leaves in a Halazone solution or 1 tsp. household bleach to 1 quart water. Rinse well before using.

Wild Rice

Zizania aquatica   **Grass Family**

Wild Rice is native to fresh-water marshes, ponds and slow-moving waters of the upper midwestern states, around the Great Lakes, as well as from Manitoba to Nova Scotia, and in Texas and Florida. In the southeastern states, it is found only in fresh-water marshes close to the coast. Attempts to plant wild rice for wildlife food have been made in Alberta, Washington, Oregon, California and Idaho.

An aquatic member of the grass family, wild rice is a reedlike plant 4 to 6 feet tall. It has leaves 4 feet long and up to 2 inches wide with very rough edges. By summer the plant is topped by a plume of flower clusters. The short-lived, pollen-bearing flowers are at the bottom of the flower cluster with the seed-bearing flowers at the top. When the seeds ripen in the fall, they look like tiny black rods encased in light-colored husks having a long, stiff hair on one end.

A canoe, rowboat or, possibly, waders are a necessity for the lucky person who finds enough wild rice to harvest. Gather by shaking the head of rice over a container, if wading; or bend the stalks over the boat or canoe, striking them hard enough to dislodge the oatlike grain. Spread to dry in a warm place low in humidity. When thoroughly dry, the husks may be removed by rubbing the seeds between the hands, or by rubbing in a sieve and blowing off the chaff.

Limited amounts of wild rice are gathered commercially, and it sells for what many consider a high price. However, this truly "wild" product, packed with natural vitamins and protein, is worth every cent. The Indians mixed wild rice with maize and other grains.

Wild Rice (*Zizania aquatica*)

33

Also try combining it with some of the pond seeds described in this book, or with domestic white or brown rice. Cooking makes the dry seeds burst forth into fluffy, whitish-gray and black kernels twice their original size. Wild rice has a delicious smoky taste that enhances fish or fowl, making an ordinary dish a gourmet's delight. Try our recipe suggestions, pages 85 and 86, or create your own taste thrills.

Wild Rice (*Zizania aquatica*)

TREES & SHRUBS

Alder

Alnus spp.   **Birch Family**

Alder (*Alnus spp.*)

At least eight species of alder grow as trees in the United States and Canada, and there are two species that are usually considered shrubs. Preferring disturbed ground, alders like moist soil and will often grow by a rock slide, an old railroad grade or an abandoned road. Although their growth is rapid, alders are short-lived. After the demise of an alder growth, evergreen forests usually follow.

The heavily veined leaves are elliptical in shape with toothed or lobed edges. In the spring, long tasseling flowers hang from the ends of the branches, and below these, small conelike strobiles ½ inch to nearly 1½ inches in length hang in clusters. The bark varies from blue-gray to brown in color and is usually smooth in young trees. The bark of the red alder has blotches of white but gets its name from the reddish brown layer called the cambium, inside the inner bark. This slippery material was scraped off and eaten fresh or dried by some Northwest Indian tribes.

Tea can be made by pouring boiling water over strips of the bark. Many other wild plants make a much superior tea, but this could make a good survival food in winter when other plants are not plentiful. The Indians used the bark as a dye and the wood of the tree for fashioning eating utensils and bowls. Alder is usually preferred where available as firewood as it does not spark. It is also valued commercially in the manufacture of furniture, veneers, and pulp products.

Bog Blueberry, Bog Bilberry
Western Blueberry, Western Huckleberry

Vaccinium occidentale   **Heath Family**

Bog Blueberry (*Vaccinium occidentale*)

The Bog Blueberry grows in bogs, swamps, ponds and grassy meadows from near sea level to the middle elevations of the Olympic Mountains and the western and eastern slopes of the Cascades; and from British Columbia southward to the Siskiyou Mountains of northern California. In California, it is also found at higher elevations (6000 to 7000 feet) in the Sierra Nevadas. Similar species grow in the tundra and muskeg of Alaska and Canada, and in cool regions across the United States. We found the one illustrated where a pond had evolved into a meadow and forest, at an elevation of 500 feet.

Bog Blueberry is known by several common names. This low-growing shrub, only about 1 to 2 feet high, could easily be overlooked among the large plants and shrubs of the bog. It has many smooth branchlets with oval, ¾-inch leaves that taper at the base and spread toward the tip. Single or pairs of round, pinkish

37

flowers, located at the axil of the leaves, appear in the spring. The sweet, many-seeded, dark-blue berries have a light waxy coating, and are usually ripe by early summer.

Raw Bog Blueberries are sweeter than their bushy relatives, making the backbreaking work of picking them and fending off mosquitoes, worthwhile. They make delicious muffins (see recipe section), pies, syrup, jellies and jams, plus other desserts. Try them in your own favorite blueberry or huckleberry recipe. (And see recipes on pages 76 and 77.)

Cottonwood

Populus trichocarpa   **Willow Family**

About fifteen species of the willow or poplar family have spotty distribution across the United States. The cottonwood is commonly found along streams and ponds throughout the West.

Generally the leaves are triangular, 2½ to 5 inches long, smooth, bright green, with light undersides, and serrated edges. The leaves on young trees can be 8 inches long, narrow and tapering. Young trees have smooth, green bark; older trees have thick, dark bark with furrowed ridges. At fruiting time the catkins are covered with soft, downy fuzz and they fill the air with cotton wisps.

The inner bark is edible on any of the many species, and makes good emergency food. The catkins may be eaten raw or boiled in stews. A sweet honey odor fills the air in the springtime from the sticky buds. This sticky substance can be used as a makeshift glue or as an ointment for cuts and scratches. May or June is the best time to try the slimy cambium, but it sours rapidly. For this reason the Indians could not store it. The trees grow up to about 160 feet tall and are cut for lumber and veneer.

Cottonwood (*Populus trichocarpa*)

39

Pacific Crabapple

Malus fusca   **Rose Family**

Sometimes called the Oregon Crabapple, this wild apple can be found in the Aleutian Islands, along the coastal region from Alaska to mid-California, and inland to the Sierra Nevadas. Crabapples prefer moist soil around ponds, beside streams, and along coastal areas.

Pacific Crabapple (*Malus fusca*)

The Pacific Crabapple is often shrublike. It grows in thickets or as a small tree up to 30 feet high, its branches covered with thorn-like spurs. Growing alternately, the deciduous oval leaves taper to a point at the tip, and some are irregularly lobed with sharply-toothed edges. The bark on older trees is rough and scaly and sometimes deeply fissured. White, flat blossoms hang in clusters through April and May. The apples are oval and about one half inch long, ripening from yellow to red in August and September.

These tart little fruits were used by the early settlers for preserves, pickles, sauces and pies. We make a tart jelly without added pectin that is delicious with meat or fowl. A few really ripe wild crabapples are good to snack on raw; however it's probably best to avoid eating very many this way. All apple seeds contain cyanide, a poison which cooking renders harmless.

Cranberry

Vaccinium Oxycoccus var. intermedium   **Heath Family**

The wild cranberry ranges from Alaska to northern California on the West Coast, and Newfoundland to Virginia on the East Coast. A careful search at the edge of a swamp or pond will reward the forager who discovers the wild or bog cranberry fruiting among soft beds of chartreuse-colored sphagnum moss. Another clue to its whereabouts is the presence of Labrador Tea and the Swamp Laurel. (See pages 44-45.)

The very slender black vines of the cranberry plant may grow as long as four feet. Small, green, sharp-pointed leaves grow alternately on the vines. Pink blossoms like shooting stars appear from late spring to July. When the berry first forms from the blossom, it appears white, then gradually changes to pink and finally to red when ripe in the early fall.

Cranberry (*Vaccinium Oxycoccus var. intermedium*)

Collected and used extensively by the Indians and the early settlers, cranberry is said to have acquired its name because the blossom resembles the head and neck of a crane. If the berries are not bruised during picking, they will keep for a long time in a cool place. Cranberries freeze well for longer storage. Wild cranberries have a more delightfully tangy flavor than commercial cranberries. They are firmer, smaller, and have a slightly tougher skin. Cranberries are very versatile and can be used to make sauce, jelly, relish, bread, juice, desserts and jello salads. (See recipes on pages 77, 78, 81 and 82.)

Gooseberry, Swamp Gooseberry

Ribes lacustre   **Saxifrage Family**

Swamp Gooseberry (*Ribes lacustre*)

Gooseberries grow coast to coast from Canada south to North Carolina and Missouri, and on the West Coast south to central California. Some of the numerous kinds of gooseberries, such as the one shown here, prefer wet soil around swamps and wetlands.

The leaves of gooseberries resemble those of maple: 5-lobed, palmate, but not sharply-toothed. In some species the leaves begin to turn color before the fruit is ripe. The blossoms of *R. lacustre* are broader than long, with rather short stamens. The berries develop in clusters, and a close look will reveal fuzz all around the berry. Nature has provided some gooseberries with a defense to protect its fruits. Swamp gooseberry has spines around its straight stems and at the nodes, so the forager must harvest these gooseberries cautiously.

Gooseberry pie has long been an American tradition. Use wild gooseberries much the same as cultivated species, by cooking them into jams, jellies, sauces or pies. They are usable either ripe, deep blue, or green. Usually high in acid and small in size, gooseberries can be combined with other fruit that is blander and sweeter to make jelly or jam without using commercial pectins. (See recipes on pages 77 and 81.)

Labrador Tea, Swamp Labrador Tea
Hudson Bay Tea, Haida Tea

Ledum groenlandicum   **Heath Family**

This aromatic shrub is found in cold marshes, sphagnum ponds, and bogs from Alaska to western Washington, western Oregon, eastward to New England, Labrador and Greenland.

Labrador Tea is an erect, branching plant, 1½ to 4 feet tall with alternate leaves spiralling around the stem. The leathery leaves are 2 to 4 inches long and elliptical in shape. Thick yellow to rusty fuzz beneath the upper rolled edges of the fragant leaf is a distinctive feature of Swamp Labrador Tea (*Ledum groenlandicum*). Compact terminal clusters of small white flowers appear June to August from large, scaly buds. The new growth of the season originates from the base of the flowers. As the leaves mature, some of them seem to grow out horizontally and others droop downward from the stems.

Swamp Labrador Tea leaves make a delightful tea. Long ago the American Indians gathered the leaves for a healthful beverage. It was also gathered for tea by the American colonists when English tea became so expensive. Pick the fresh young leaves and dry on trays in a very low oven. For variety in flavor, let the leaves brown slightly. A dehydrator may be used for drying, or place on trays on high beams near the ceiling. Store dried leaves in airtight containers.

Swamp Labrador Tea (*Ledum groenlandicum*)

To prepare, crush about 1 tablespoon per cup into a tea ball and drop into boiling water. Let steep for about five minutes. For variety, combine with dried mint leaves or other teas. Add honey or lemon to taste. As a refreshing change, chew on some leaves while hunting, hiking or fishing.

Warning: Be sure to correctly identify this plant before using. Two closely related shrubs, Mountain Labrador Tea (*Ledum grandulosum*) and Swamp Laurel (*Kalmia polifolia*) are toxic in concentrated amounts. These two plants are often found growing with Swamp Labrador Tea (*Ledum groenlandicum*) which is not toxic. The growth form of both plants is similar, but the major difference is that the leaves of Mountain Labrador Tea (*Ledum grandulosum*) and Swamp Laurel (*Kalmia polifolia*) do not have thick yellow fuzz beneath the leaves. Swamp Laurel has lavender-pink blossoms.

Mountain Labrador Tea
(Ledum grandulosum)
POISON

Swamp Laurel
(Kalmia polifolia)
POISON

Salmonberry

Rubus spectabilis   **Rose Family**

The big, juicy salmonberry is found in swamps, stream banks, moist woods, and even in mountain areas below 3000 feet, from Alaska to California and Idaho.

This deciduous shrub grows to 6 or 8 feet tall. The glossy brown, usually erect stems have shreddy yellow bark and may bear weak thorns. Fuzzy, saw-toothed leaflets, separated usually into three parts, measure about 3 inches across. The fuchsia-red flowers appear almost before the leaves from March to June, depending on the altitude. This rather bland fruit varies in color from bright yellow to red. Indians considered the fruit too soft to dry, but they did eat it fresh. Speculation has it that the name came either from the color of the fruit or the fact that the Pacific Northwest Indians steamed the tender young shoots to eat along with their dried salmon.

Salmonberries make a beautiful, delicious jelly that combines well with meats, especially beef and pork. The fruit deteriorates rapidly, so it must be used as soon as possible after picking. And pick plenty of leaves for Salmonberry tea! (See recipes on pages 76 and 78.)

Salmonberry (*Rubus spectabilis*)

Squashberry, Highbush Cranberry

Viburnum edule   **Honeysuckle Family**

Squashberries of this species can be found in parts of British Columbia, in the Cascade Mountains of Washington and Oregon, and in boggy ponds throughout the West, including the Rocky Mountains. We found them in wet, boggy soil surrounding sub-alpine ponds of coastal areas around the Olympic Mountains. Another squashberry species has similar fruit but larger, more showy blooms, and prefers drier soil.

Squashberry (*Viburnum edule*)

Autumn is the best time of the year to search for the berries, but look for the 2- to 3-inch clusters of small white flowers by midsummer. Usually hidden among Wild Crabapple and Red Osier Dogwood, you will find this scraggly shrub 3 to 8 feet tall with smooth, reddish bark. Its crinkly, opposite-growing leaves are usually 3-lobed, but they are variable and may be without lobes. In the fall, squashberry suddenly displays gorgeous crimson leaves and clusters of bright red berries. These juicy, tart berries have one large flat seed. Wait for a frost to make them sweet and more palatable. The berries hang on the bushes long after the leaves have fallen off, providing food for birds.

These berries eaten raw are good thirst quenchers when hiking or fishing the ponds. Pick some to take home with you as they make a delicious jelly to serve with meats. Combine with a less acid fruit to save on sugar. (See recipe on page 79.)

Black Twinberry

Lonicera involucrata   **Honeysuckle Family**

Black Twinberry (*Lonicera involucrata*)

The Black Twinberry grows east and west of the Cascade Mountains from British Columbia to northern California, in the wet areas around ponds, lakes, and along the seacoast from sea level to mountain slopes.

Not well-known, but nonetheless abundant, this shrub may stand 2 to 10 feet high. The stems are straw-colored and appear square and coarse. Some have fine hairs on them and others do not. The oval leaves, 2 to 4 inches long, are a shiny light green color and grow opposite on the branch. From the axil of the leaf, on an approximately 2-inch stem, grow two separate yellow flowers which bloom by May or June. These blossoms are replaced by pairs of shiny, black, oblong berries on a red "ruff" usually by July or August. These pairs suggest its name, Twinberry.

Indian tribes had various names for this berry that suggested which animals ate them, but apparently none thought of the twinberry as edible for humans. This is a sweet berry that can be consumed raw, made into syrup for hot cakes or waffles, or made into jelly. Combine with a more acid berry like Squashberry to improve the flavor. (See also recipes on pages 76 and 78.)

Wild Rose

Rosa spp.   **Rose Family**

The wild rose is recognized as a familiar deciduous shrub growing almost everywhere in North America. It has been around for a long time: fossil specimens found in the West date back thirty-five million years! Preferring wet soil, swamp roses, *Rosa pisocarpa*, often form thickets around ponds and along streams. *Rosa nutkana* is a common species growing along roadsides, shorelines, meadows, and in the woods.

Swamp Rose (*Rosa pisocarpa*)

The usually smooth and glossy saw-toothed leaflets are five to seven to a leaf. Clusters of up to six small, pale to bright pink flowers beautify the pond or swamp from May to July. After the flowers die, seed pods, known as hips, are formed. Usually these ripen in August, and in some places they hang onto the bushes throughout winter and are still usable. These erect shrubs have spiny or thorny stems and usually grow in dense, sometimes impenetrable thickets.

Used extensively by the Greeks before the birth of Christ, rose petals were made into puddings and wines. And they were said to have been placed into other wines to prevent drunkenness.
50

Generally, the rose hips are the part of the plant consumed now, but the petals are useful for making tea, salads, jellies, candies, and wine. Concentrated rose hips have 400% more Vitamin C than oranges, plus Vitamins A and P. When consumed raw, some hips taste like fresh apples. Substitute cut-up hips in the cranberry bread recipe (page 76), use fresh in a salad, or prepare for tea. Rose hips make a superb, delicate after-dinner wine. Any way you use them, you are receiving the healthful benefits of Vitamin C, which is recognized for its many uses in addition to the prevention of colds. (See recipes on pages 80 and 81.)

Wild Rose (*Rosa spp.*)

Willow

Salix spp.   **Willow Family**

The willow is common throughout North America. From sea level to timberline, more than 100 species are native. Most willows prefer moist to wet ground.

Willows are deciduous trees or shrubs with very narrow tapering leaves that grow alternately along the branches. Bees obtain nectar from the catkin blossoms in early spring, produced as male and female catkins on separate plants. The color of willow bark ranges from browns and greys to black.

The edible part of the willow is the inner bark, but it is bitter and rates only as an emergency food. The bark can be dried and ground into flour to make it more edible. Some of the fine branches are used in basketmaking, and the pussy willows make popular dried floral arrangements.

Willow (*Salix spp.*)

ANIMALS

Largemouth Bass

Micropterus salmoides

Common In fresh-water ponds, lakes and slugglsh streams, the Largemouth Bass is a member of the sunfish family, and is found throughout North America, especially in the central and southern regions. These same areas have other species of fresh-water bass,

Bass (*Micropterus salmoides*)

such as Smallmouth Bass; White Crappie, also called White Bass; Black Crappie, also known as Calico Bass; and Strawberry Bass or Grass Bass (not shown).

Largemouth Bass are usually bigger than their relatives, averaging 4 to 8 pounds, weighing up to even 22 pounds in the South. As their common name implies, they have a large mouth with a protruding lower jaw. Young ones may have dark blotches on yellow-green sides with a whitish underbelly. Older bass tend to be dark green to black. They feed on smaller fish and other animals. Fishing for this wily creature is a popular sport with anglers who try to entice them with live fish, frogs, worms, or with specially-designed plugs and plastic worm lures. Use slightly heavier tackle for bass than for trout.

Each species of fresh-water bass has flaky, tender, and tasty flesh. To prepare for cooking see our advice in the recipe section, pages 87 and 88.

Bluegill, Bream, Sunfish, Pumpkinseed, Panfish

Leponis macrochirus

Bluegills and other species of the widespread sunfish family are found in clear, fresh-water ponds and lakes throughout North America. The members of this family of scaly, flat, brightly-colored fish are well-known. They are called by various names, some unprintable, when caught by anglers fishing for other, so-called "sportier" fish. The roundish Bluegill Sunfish has blue-green gills, a dark green back, and upper sides with darker markings. Lower sides are yellow, shading to orange beneath the pectoral fins. It averages 6 to 8 inches in length, but a 12-inch, 1-pound sunfish has been caught, and considered a giant! Recently established, the record Washington State Pumpkinseed Sunfish catch was 12 ounces in weight and 9 inches in length. The estimated age of the fish was 7 years.

Bluegill (*Leponis macrochirus*)

A large female Bluegill may lay over 60,000 eggs at one spawning, and although only a few of the young survive, they can soon overstock a small pond. Since they feed on insects, crustaceans, and

55

other small animals, they can be caught easily by even a novice using worms for bait with light fishing gear. Little fighters, they deserve a higher rating both as a game and food fish; a quarter-pounder will put up as much fight per ounce as any game fish. Small Bluegills are best if scaled before cooking. The flesh is flaky, sweet and delicious. (See the recipe section, pages 87 and 88.)

Catfish, Bullheads

Ictalurus spp.

Catfish (*Ictalurus spp.*)

Catfish can be found in fresh-water ponds and sluggish streams throughout North America. Members of the spiny group of fish considered by some people as scrap fish, these edibles have been poisoned by some game departments, supposedly to make room for game fish such as trout.

The very common bullhead types of catfish are usually small with square-cut tail fins. The large Channel Catfish, which can weigh well over 40 pounds, and Blue Catfish have forked tail fins. All have barbels, or whiskers, around their mouths, which are sensory organs to aid in finding food. All catfish also have sharp spines in their pectoral and dorsal fins. These spines in some of the smaller species are poisonous and can cause painful injuries if not handled carefully. Most catfish have no scales on their thick rubbery skin. Catfish feed on small bottom creatures and waste matter, making the water cleaner for other fish. Since they are nocturnal feeders, nighttime is considered the best time to fish; however, "cats" will bite almost any kind of bait at any time of day. They have been known to make a grunting sound on cloudy days and evenings. (See recipes, pages 87 and 88.)

Clams & Mussels

Class: *Bivalvia*

Fresh-water clams and mussels live in the mud and sand of ponds, lakes and streams. They are rarely found in water over six feet deep. The ones pictured are commonly found throughout the western United States. Pearly mussel, *Elliptio crassidens*, is common to eastern North America and is especially abundant in the Mississippi Valley. We have found mussels and clams in the White River, Indiana, a tributary of the Wabash.

Clams (*Bivalvia*)   Mussels (*Bivalvia*)

Fresh-water clams and mussels have a hinged, two-part shell and two tubelike openings or siphons which may be found protruding out of the pond or lake bottom. The other end has a wedge-shaped foot that can burrow into mud or sand. Water containing food and oxygen is siphoned in through one tube by cilia, and the animal's waste is carried out through the other tube. Adults carry up to three million eggs. When these hatch, the baby clams and mussels attach themselves to gills or fins of fish, where they live as parasites until mature enough to drop to the muddy bottoms of ponds, lakes or streams. Unlike their salt-water relatives who attach themselves to rocks by a collection of silky filaments called a byssus, fresh-water mussels are mobile.

Depending on the species, the green, brownish or black outer shell can be thick or thin, with a pearly inside, colored pink, peach, lavender or white. When polished, the shells are very decorative and are often used for buttons and ornaments. The age of plastics may have saved these bivalves from extinction, for they are no longer gathered in quantity for the button industry.

We suggest opening the shells by pouring hot water over them. Be careful not to chip the shell when prying open, for a shell collector might treasure it. First remove the digestive organs and rinse well in cold water. Try your favorite salt-water clam recipes using fresh-water clams and mussels. (And see recipes on pages 88 and 89.) **Never** eat them raw. Unfortunately they can and sometimes do live in polluted water. If you think by the smell or the appearance of the water that it may be polluted, do not collect these bivalves in that area. Search out the unpolluted pond, lake or stream for these delectable creatures.

Crayfish, Crawfish, Crawdad

Cambarus spp.

Crayfish (*Cambarus spp.*)

There are over 200 species of crayfish living in the fresh waters of North America, some of which can survive in wet soil. Not fish, crayfish are crustaceans with eight legs and two long antennae which protrude from the front of the head. In addition to using the legs, locomotion is also accomplished by flipping a powerful tail underneath the body; this moves the animal backwards at a rapid speed. They are equipped with two vicious claws that act as effective tools to tear apart food.

Crayfish avoid the currents in the water by hiding beneath rocks and stones. Since they feed on plants and animals both living and dead, they help to clean up organic pollutants in streams and ponds. They in turn become food for turtles, fish, herons and other birds, and mammals. The female carries her eggs beneath her body. After these relatively large eggs hatch, the young crayfish cling to the mother for protection until they are large enough to survive on their own.

An agile person may grab the crayfish by the tail where water is not too deep, or in the wet earth. Deeper waters may require a trap or a net. To prepare for eating, drop the animal alive in boiling salted water (¼ cup salt to 1 quart water). Boil about 10 minutes, remove, and immerse quickly in cold water. Drain and cool. Break off the only edible part, the tail. When very large, cut nearly through the thick part of the meat, to make a butterfly shape. This way it will cook more evenly when deep fat frying. Crayfish may be substituted in recipes calling for lobster, shrimp or prawns. The taste is quite similar, and some restaurants have been known to serve crayfish when the menu advertised prawns. (See also the recipe on page 90.)

Mallard Ducks

Anas platyrhynchos

Mallards are the most abundant of all wild ducks. Inhabiting fresh-water marshes and ponds of northern Asia, Europe and North America, they seem to prefer marshy land near streams flowing into salt water. Some are permanent residents, while others migrate north in the spring and come back to rejoin flocks in the winter.

Mallard Ducks (*Anas platyrhynchos*)

Mallards average about 2 feet in length. The drake (male) has curly tail feathers, is greyish-brown on the back, purplish-chestnut on the underside, and has an iridescent greenish-blue head and neck. The wings are marked with two white and two black bars, and a white band encircles the neck. This distinctive coloring of the drake is brightest while he is courting. Usually the greyish-brown female builds her down-lined nest of grass and weeds on the ground or on a low-growing branch. She lays a clutch of 6 to 13 olive-colored eggs that take about a month to hatch. Although the drake may be the most beautiful, mother nature gave the female the voice in the family. She does all the loud quacking while all he can produce is a low grunt or whistle.

Mallard ducks feed mostly on plant life in shallow water or dry land, but they do eat some small aquatic animals. They are typical "dabbling" ducks because they reach their food on the bottom by dipping from the surface instead of diving. Since they are not primarily fish eaters, like diving ducks, they are considered choice eating and are often hunted for food. If you can kill this beautiful creature, we have some hints on preparation and cooking in the recipe section, page 90.

FROGS

Bullfrog

Rana catesbeiana

Bullfrogs are seldom on dry land. They prefer to live among the plants of ponds, lakes and slow-moving streams that have deep, soft, muddy bottoms. They are found in most parts of the United States and in Europe.

Bullfrog (*Rana catesbeiana*)

The largest of the many frogs in the United States, bullfrogs have greenish-yellow, olive-green or brown-red bodies banded with black on their hind legs. A distinctive feature is the round eardrum, which is larger than the eye. All frogs have a mating call, but the male bullfrog's call, which sounds to us like "go-around," is unique. From early spring well into summer, he starts calling for a mate at nightfall. The female is voiceless. She may lay up to 20,000 black and white eggs which take 5 to 20 days to hatch into tadpoles. It takes the tadpoles 2 years to grow to 6 inches. They then turn into frogs of only about 2 inches. After several years they reach their full length of about 8 inches, with the hind legs reaching 10 inches. They can weigh several pounds; but because of many predators such as fish, snakes, large birds and mammals, few ever reach full maturity. Man is now probably the bullfrog's greatest predator, the annual catch for food in the United States being several million pounds per year.

Not only is the bullfrog useful as a source of food, but it is helpful also, as its diet chiefly consists of insects. It also eats snails, crawfish and small invertebrates. Bullfrogging can be a challenging sport, as these wily amphibians can hop 5 feet or more.

Fried frog legs are considered high-class fare. Most frog "hunters" have their favorite weapons for frogging. A bright light and a 3-pronged barbless gig made of high-quality steel is highly recommended in areas where it is legal. A bright beam of light shone on the frog can cause a hypnotizing effect, sometimes making it possible to net or pick up the quarry. Some hunters say the best time for frogging is 10 P.M. to 2 A.M. A piece of red yarn attached to a hook and line on a fish pole is a common lure in the daytime.

The hind legs of bullfrogs are the parts most commonly used for food. In Germany, a stew is made using all the frog, after it is cleaned. In the recipe section we have given suggestions on preparation and cooking, page 90.

Leopard Frog, Meadow Frog

Rana pipiens

The leopard frog inhabits shallow ponds and wet areas, often straying to grassy meadows during the summer. It is probably the most common frog in North America, especially through the Midwestern United States.

This amphibian has greenish-gold skin covered with rounded black spots. A raised light line extends along the body from the back of each eye. In the spring after hibernation, the male leopard frog has a mating call that sounds to us like he's saying "too deep, too deep." Meanwhile the bullfrog is saying "go-around, go-around" with his distinctive call. Leopard or meadow frogs are much smaller than bullfrogs. It takes them also a few years to reach maturity and to weigh half a pound. During their growth period, frogs shed their skin several times. The skin splits down the back, and the frog pulls the old skin over its head. Many frogs eat their old skin.

65

Frogs develop large hind legs for swimming and for jumping on land. We can vouch for a leopard frog's ability to jump 15 feet in one leap. They are an asset to have living in a pond because their principal diet is insects, besides furnishing mighty good eating. A dip net is the best way to catch these amphibians, and they have been gathered and sold commercially for food. The legs are small, so it takes several leopard frogs for a meal. They are just as incredibly delicious as bullfrogs. See the recipe section for cleaning and cooking hints, page 90.

Leopard Frog (*Rana pipiens*)

Canada Goose

Branta canadensis

The well-known Canada Goose, of which there are many kinds, lives in marshy areas, ponds and lakes of North America. This large close relative of the duck and swan, breeds in Canada and flies south in autumn as far as Mexico. It is also found in Britain and Sweden.

Belonging to the group called "black" geese, the Canada Goose has a wing span of about 6 feet. Its head, neck and tail are black, and it has a white strap around its throat. Near the tail is a gland that produces an oil with which the goose uses its beak to waterproof its feathers. The gander (male) and goose (the female is called just "goose") both look alike in all kinds of geese. They build down- or feather-lined nests of grass on marshy ground. Wild geese usually lay 3 to 6 white eggs. When migrating, they fly rapidly in great V-shaped formations, honking loudly. They have been known to fly more than 29,000 feet above sea level—higher than Mount Everest! Normally geese live a long life, as much as 30 years in captivity. Strict conservation should ensure that these unique birds, which have been cited in ancient histories, will remain with us.

Canada Goose (*Branta canadensis*)

Canada Geese eat grain and other plant life, but sometimes feed on insects and small aquatic animals. They tend to feed in wide-open water and marshes, making it difficult for hunters to get near. While feeding, these cautious and intelligent birds seem to post sentries to warn the rest of the flocks of any possible danger. The wild Canada Goose is usually not as fat as a domestic goose, but can be a gourmet's delight, prepared and stuffed with wild rice. If ever lucky enough to get a young gander, try our recipe for it (page 90).

Rainbow Trout	*Salmo gairdneri*
Steelhead Trout	*Salmo gairdneri*
Cutthroat Trout	*Salmo clarki*
Brook Trout	*Salvelinus fontinalis*

Rainbow and Cutthroat Trout naturally inhabit clear, cold, freshwater ponds, lakes, and streams in western North America, and also have been introduced to the cold waters of eastern North America, Europe and New Zealand.

Rainbow Trout (*Salmo gairdneri*)

Not true trout, Rainbows belong to the salmon family. They are sleek, streamlined fish with a wide pinkish-violet band along each side. Their fins and body are covered with small dark dots. The average weight of a Rainbow is 1 to 2 pounds, but they can weigh as much as 40 pounds. Steelhead Trout (not pictured) are the same species as Rainbow, only they inhabit rivers and spend part of their life at sea.

Cutthroat Trout (again incorrectly named) belong also to the salmon family. These colorful fish can be distinguished by the pink mark on the throat with small dark dots on the fins and body. The size of Cutthroats varies from a few ounces to several pounds.

Cutthroat Trout (*Salmo clarki*)

Brook Trout (*Salvelinus fontinalis*)

Brook Trout belong to the char family, which are close relatives of the salmon. These colorful fish are also not true trout. Brook Trout vary in color, with brownish, green, or gold sides covered with bright round dots. The front edges of the fins are edged with white.

All of these species of so-called trout feed on insects, mussels, clams, crustaceans, and other fishes. Catching them challenges the skill of most anglers, who try to entice these popular fish to bite lures resembling flies. Nightcrawlers and other worms are also used as bait.

Incredibly edible is the best way to describe all freshly prepared trout. Always clean fish in preparation for cooking as soon as possible after catching. (See recipe section for hints on cleaning and cooking, pages 87 and 88.)

Painted Turtle
Snapping Turtle
Softshell Turtle

Chrysemys picta
Chelydra serpentina
Trionyx muticus

The Painted Turtle ranges widely from the East Coast to eastern Washington; the Snapping Turtle and Softshell Turtle are widespread from the Rockies to the East Coast and Canada. Their many relatives are found world-wide.

Turtles are living fossils. They belong to an ancient group of animals that were entirely land-dwelling reptiles some 200 million years ago. Where winters are cold, turtles hibernate in the mud at the bottom of ponds, and during hot, dry weather some become dormant. They can be found migrating across land, especially during breeding season. All turtles lay eggs, burying them in the ground. Given the chance, they may live 150 years, longer than any other animal. They can protect themselves from danger by retreating into their shell-like armor. This armor consists of a top shell, called the carapace, with a lower shell beneath the body, called the plastron. Turtles eat some plants, but live mostly on insects, worms, and shellfish, or by scavenging. Although they are toothless, they can efficiently rip and tear apart plant and animal life with their beaklike

Painted Turtle (*Chrysemys picta*)

Snapping Turtle (*Chelydra serpentina*)

Softshell Turtle (*Trionyx muticus*)

mouth. They generally have shy, placid dispositions. However, always handle any turtle carefully in case it tries to bite, especially the snapper. This one always seems to be in a bad mood, and will snap at anything or anyone that gets near it. Always handle a snapper by the tail, for its head can reach and snap almost anywhere around its carapace. In case of being bit, experts advise keeping calm. Usually the bill can be pried open to release the trapped part without much injury.

In certain areas where some species of turtles are plentiful, they are gathered commercially for food and considered quite a delicacy. However, check the turtle population before taking the life of these harmless creatures. See recipe section for how to clean and cook, page 91.

RECIPES

Sample Menus

Turtle and Wild Rice Delight
Cattail Ears with melted butter
Watercress Salad tossed with vinegar and oil dressing
Pollen Muffins
Rose Hip syrup drizzled over champagne ice cream
Labrador-Mint Tea

Roast Wild Duck or Goose
Wild Rice stuffing
Sweet Potato-Cranberry Bake
Nettles served with vinegar and butter
Wild Cranberry molded jello salad
Bog Berry pie or tarts served with dollop of cream

(Because these are not all ripe at the same time, we are assuming you will be freezing your berries and nettles for use when you need them.)

BEVERAGES

Refreshing Berry Cooler

1 C berries (salmon, twinberry, bogberry, blackberry, etc.)
2 C milk
1 T lemon juice (less for tart berries)
1 to 3 T sugar (again depending on tartness)
Ice cubes if desired.

For seedy berries such as salmonberries, put berries through juicer first, then add ingredients as listed in the blender, or hand mix.

Salmonberry-Mint Tea

Salmonberry makes a beautiful, delectable jelly, but one should not overlook the leaves as a source of tea. Collect clean-looking leaves of both mint and salmonberry that grow away from the highway. Wash thoroughly and dry in an open oven at low heat, in the sun, or any dry area. A beam near the ceiling of the kitchen can make a good drying spot. Crush thoroughly when dry and store in tightly sealed jar. When ready to use, fill your tea caddy and drop into warmed teapot. Pour on freshly boiled water and let seep for 5 minutes. Combine with other teas if desired.

MUFFINS, PIES & SWEETS

Cattail Pollen Muffins

Gather cattails when heads are mature in late August or September. Tap heads and yellow pollen will fall out, bits of fibre also. All parts are edible.

1 C cake flour	¾ t salt
1 C pollen (pick 10-16 heads)	¼ C sugar
3 t baking powder	

Sift these ingredients. To this add:

2 eggs, beaten	2 T melted butter
¾ C milk	

Mix with 15 strokes and put into greased muffin tins. Bake 15 to 20 minutes at 400° F.

Blueberry Muffins

1 C blueberries	1 C white flour
1 C milk	1 t salt
¼ C oil	1 C whole wheat flour
⅓ C sugar	3 t baking powder
1 egg	

Combine egg, milk and oil. Gradually add to dry ingredients. Stir only until all the flour is moist. Gently fold in berries. Fill muffin cups ⅔ full. Bake 20 minutes at 400° F.

Wild Cranberry Bread

Juice of 2 oranges (add enough water to make 1¾ cups)

2 T margarine	½ t cloves
2 T grated orange rind	½ t allspice
3 C white flour	½ t ginger
1 t soda	1 C whole wheat flour
1½ t baking powder	2 eggs beaten slightly
1 t cinnamon	½ C flour
1 t nutmeg	3 C cranberries
1 t salt	2 C walnuts
2 C sugar	

(NOTE: Try crushing seeds from sedges, grasses, and/or bulreeds and add to flour for variety.)

Bring orange juice and water to boil; add margarine and orange rind. Cool. Sift white flour, measure, sift again with dry ingredients. Combine whole wheat flour and white flour mixture. Make a well in flour mixture, pour in cooled fruit mixture. Mix, add eggs, stir gently. Sprinkle ½ cup flour over cranberries and nuts, blend carefully into flour mixture. Line 2 loaf pans with foil, oil well. Bake at 350° for 1½ hours or until done; test with toothpick.

Gooseberry Pie

1 C sugar	1 T flour
2 C gooseberries	1 T butter

Pie dough for 2 crust pie

Place the sugar, berries, flour and butter in a bowl and mix well. Pour into unbaked pie shell and cover with top crust. Make slits in crust. Bake in 425° oven for about 35 minutes.

Mock Strawberry Shortcake (Cranberries)

Grind one cup of raw cranberries twice, saving the juice. Add to 1 cup grated peeled apple, 1 cup crushed pineapple and 1 cup sugar. Place in refrigerator for several hours. Use over any shortcake and top with dollop of cream. Tiny cranberry seeds make it look like strawberries and it tastes remarkably like the "real" thing.

Sweet Potato and Cranberry Bake

4 large sweet potatoes (may substitute any wild tubers)
½ C brown sugar
1 t butter or margarine
1 C fresh wild cranberries
½ C orange juice

Cook, cool and peel sweet potatoes. Cut into ¼-inch slices. Arrange potatoes in greased 1½ qt. casserole and sprinkle with ¼ cup brown sugar. Dot with butter and sprinkle ½ cup cranberries over it. Layer remaining sweet potatoes, sprinkle with remaining brown sugar and cranberries. Pour juice over top. Cover and bake in 350° oven for 45 minutes. Uncover, distribute topping over casserole and bake 10 minutes longer.

WALNUT TOPPING: In a small bowl combine ½ cup chopped walnuts or wild nuts, 2 tablespoons melted butter or margarine, 1 tablespoon brown sugar and ½ teaspoon cinnamon.

Fruit Leather

Purée raw or cooked bogberry, twinberry, crabapple, or salmonberry, sweeten to taste with honey or sugar. (If using berries with large seeds, rub purée through a sieve.)

Spray cookie sheet with a cookware coating; pour fruit on sheet to desired thickness. Place in oven set at warm for about 24 hours or until it feels dry. Brace the oven door open an inch during drying. Cut into sections and roll up. Store in freezer—it takes about 10 minutes to thaw enough to eat.

When using fruits such as peaches, pears, apricots and apples, add ascorbic acid to the purée to prevent color loss.

Seed & Nut Energy Bars (Burreed, Rushes, Sedges)

With a portable oven, you may be able to make these at the campsite. If not, collect your grass seeds and wild nuts to use for these healthful cookies when you return home. You will need:

12 T margarine	A few grains of salt
1½ C brown sugar	1 C seeds or nuts, finely ground
1 egg	1¼ C whole wheat flour

Melt the butter in a saucepan. Remove from heat and stir in sugar, then egg and salt. Add flour and seeds; stir until well blended. Grease a 10 x 12 pan and pour evenly, flatten with back of spoon. Bake at 375° for 10 minutes. Cut into bars and remove when cool enough to hold together.

JELLIES, SAUCES & SYRUPS

Squashberry Jelly

4 C juice (made by straining about 2 quarts ripe squashberries, cooked and strained through jelly bag or cheesecloth)

6 C sugar

1 box powdered pectin

Boil juice and pectin for 1 minute in large sauce pan, stirring often. Add sugar, bring mixture to full, rolling boil for two minutes. Pour at once into hot, sterilized jars. Seal with lids or with melted paraffin

Mint Jelly

Both the powdered and liquid varieties of pectin have recipes for making fresh mint jelly. Use the wild mint for a great flavor treat. The recipes are primarily the same and call for 1½ or 1¾ cup tightly packed mint leaves and stems. Crush in pan and add water (about 3 cups). Bring to a boil. Remove from heat and let stand for 10 minutes. Strain. Add water if needed to make desired amount for recipe.

3 cups mint water with 8 drops green food coloring

1 box powdered pectin

Bring to boiling point. Add 4 cups sugar. Bring to a second boiling point and let boil for one minute, stirring occasionally. Remove from heat. Skim carefully with metal spoon and pour into glasses. This makes a beautiful jelly as well as a delicious one. Traditionally served with lamb, mint jelly is refreshing with all kinds of meats.

Mint Marinade

½ C red wine
½ C red wine vinegar
⅓ C water
3 cloves garlic, minced
½ C minced onion

30 mint leaves, chopped
⅛ t salt
¼ t sweet basil leaves
¼ t marjoram

Combine and let stand several hours or overnight. Use as marinade for meat. Makes 1½ cups.

Rose Hip Purée

Remove the stems and blossom ends of the rose hips, and wash in cold water. Put hips in a pan with enough water to cover. Bring to a boil and simmer until soft, about 10 to 15 minutes. Do not overcook. Put entire mass through a blender or rub through a sieve. Store in freezer. The purée may be used in many ways, for instance, it is delicious sweetened with honey for a spread on muffins or toast, as a sauce when sweetened or made into fruit leather (see page 78).

NOTE: Rose hips should not be cooked in an aluminum or copper pan, for the metal will destroy the Vitamin C. Always use stainless steel, cast iron, glass, or earthenware pans.

Rose Hip Sauce

Simmer rose hips until tender. Crush and put through a sieve. May be added to apple sauce or combined with sugar and used alone. Add cinnamon and/or lemon for flavor.

Rose Hip Syrup

Prepare rose hips as for purée, adding slightly more water. To this thinner purée add one part honey or corn syrup to two parts rose hip purée.

Scented Pond Lily leaves may be substituted for rose hips, but you may need to increase the amount of honey.

1 quart fresh gooseberries
1 C water
1 T butter
1 T mint leaves, finely chopped

1 T honey or sugar
pinch of nutmeg
salt

Simmer berries in water until mushy. Drain and put through sieve. Add other ingredients. Bring back to simmer and leave on for another 8 to 10 minutes. Serve hot or cold with fish, such as trout, bass, sunfish or catfish balls.

Cranberry Catsup

2½ pounds cranberries
Vinegar to cover
2⅔ C sugar

1 stick cinnamon
1 t cloves

Wash cranberries, cover with vinegar and cook until berries burst. Force through sieve. Add other ingredients and simmer until thick. Remove cinnamon, and bottle in clear jars. Either seal or store in freezer or refrigerator.

SALADS

Wapato and Burreed Salad

Wash and slice into pieces the tender inside base of leaves and stems of Burreed. Combine with sliced tubers of Wapato. Toss with oil and vinegar and favorite seasonings. Serve topped with Burreed seeds.

Cranberry & Rose Hip Salad (24 hour)

1 C raw cranberries ground
3 C tiny marshmallows
¾ C sugar
2 C diced rose hips (remove seeds)

½ C seedless green grapes
½ C broken walnuts
dash of salt
1 C cream or ½ pint, whipped

Combine berries, marshmallows and sugar. Cover and chill overnight. Add hips, walnuts and salt. Fold in whipped cream. Chill in serving bowl. Trim with fresh mint. Makes about 8 servings. Can be used as a salad or a dessert.

Save the seeds you removed from the rose hips. Crush and use the pulp as a nutritious additive to other casseroles or use for seeds in seed cookie recipes.

Watercress Potato Salad

4 or 5 medium potatoes

⅓ C or less minced green onions

2 hard-boiled eggs

3 mild radishes cut up small for color

1 bunch watercress

Pickle Dressing: (Mix together)

½ C mayonnaise or salad dressing

¼ C pickle juice

¾ t salt

½ t of fresh ground pepper

Dash of fresh lemon

Boil potatoes until tender. Drain, cool, peel and cut into pieces. Add onions, eggs, radishes and enough dressing to coat well. Toss gently. Refrigerate until cool. Just before serving, chop watercress, add to salad with the remainder of the dressing. Serves 4 to 6.

Molded Cranberry Salad

1 9 oz. can crushed pineapple

1 3 oz. package cherry jello

1 T lemon juice

½ C sugar

1 small unpeeled orange ground in a food grinder
   (using the fine blade)

1 C ground fresh cranberries
   (also using the fine blade)

1 C finely chopped celery

½ C chopped walnuts

Dissolve jello and sugar in one cup boiling water. Drain pineapple. Reserve the syrup and add enough water to make ½ cup. Add syrup and lemon juice to jello. Chill until partially set. Add cranberries, orange, celery and nuts. Pour into individual molds and chill overnight. Serve with lettuce and mayonnaise. Makes enough for 8 people.

CEREALS

Grasses, Sedges or Rushes

Thoroughly dry seeds, remove hulls if desired. Bring to boil 2 cups water, ½ teaspoon salt. Gradually add 1 cup seeds. When mixture boils, reduce heat and, stirring occasionally, cook for 30 minutes. Serve with honey or sugar and cream.

GREENS & RICE

Steamed or Boiled Wapato

Place freshly washed tubers in a steamer or a small amount of water. Cook only until tender, about 10 minutes. Season with butter, salt and pepper. Serve with meats.

NOTE: Wapato tubers, naturally rich in starch, protein and minerals can be a substitute for Irish potatoes in recipes calling for potatoes (such as potato salad), creamed with vegetables in a casserole, or stir-fried with vegetables.

Steamed or Boiled Roots — Grasses, Sedges or Rushes

Wash and scrape roots. Place in saucepan with steamer or in a minimum of water. Cook over medium heat until tender. Serve warm with butter, salt and pepper.

For the outdoor cook, wrap roots in foil with a dab of butter, salt and pepper. Bake over hot coals until tender.

Stir-Fried Sedge

Gather young tender sedge or rush stems just above roots; also gather young leaves. This must be done quite early in the spring. Slice stems and chop leaves into bite-size pieces.

1 C sedge stems and leaves, chopped	2 T cooking oil
1 C celery, sliced	1 to 2 T soy sauce
1 C onion, chopped	

Heat oil in wok or fry pan over moderate heat. Add vegetables one at a time, keeping each separate. Sauté for about 5 minutes; vegetables should be crisp. Sprinkle with soy sauce and serve at once.

Cooked Nettles

With rubber gloves wash fresh young nettle plants or shoots in several waters or under running cold water, making sure the greens are free of sand and bugs. Place in a heavy kettle over medium heat; cook about 5 minutes or until just tender. (They will wilt down, so kettle can be packed full.) After cooking starts, shift and turn the greens with a fork. Cook in a minimum of water; usually enough water clings to greens from washing. They also can be placed in a steamer. Always save the cooking liquid for soups or stews. Serve like spinach or other greens, with butter, salt and pepper, lemon juice or vinegar. (For the novice, do not worry about the "sting," cooking destroys it.)

Frozen Nettles

After washing tender young nettles well, wearing gloves, blanch by placing them in boiling water for 3 minutes. Drain and chill immediately in ice water. Do only one pint or quart at a time. Freeze at once in airtight containers. To serve, cook in about ¼ cup boiling water only a few minutes after thawed. Serve like spinach or use in any spinach recipe.

Nettles Soufflé

Combine: 2 C chopped nettles, thorougly drained
         1 C white sauce
         3 well-beaten egg yolks
         Onion, salt and pepper to taste

Fold in 3 stiffly beaten egg whites. Set in pan of warm water. Bake in moderate oven (375° F.) until inserted knife comes out clean. Approximately 6 servings.

To make white sauce, melt 2 tablespoons butter or margarine in pan, gradually stir in 2 tablespoons flour until smooth. Add one cup milk gradually until thick and bubbly.

HINT: Don't throw away the nettles juice as it makes a delicious drink combined with a little melted butter.

Basic Wild Rice

⅔ C wild rice, uncooked

3 C water

½ t salt

Run cold water through wild rice in a colander until water runs clear. Place rice in a saucepan with 3 cups cold water and ½ teaspoon salt. Bring to a boil for 1 minute, then lower temperature and simmer for 45 minutes or until rice is tender. Rinse in colander under cold water. To serve plain, add 3 tablespoons of butter, with salt and pepper. (Soaking 12 to 24 hours before cooking increases volume of wild rice.)

Mrs. K's Wild Rice

Cover about ⅓ cup wild rice with 3 cups cold water. Bring to a boil, then discard water. Do this 3 times.

Combine with 1 can cream of mushroom soup, 1 can onion soup mix, and 1 cup water. Preheat oven to 375°; place rice mixture in a covered 2 quart casserole. Bake covered for 45 minutes, remove cover and bake for 15 to 20 minutes longer. Serves four generously.

Fried Wild Rice

⅓ C wild rice

Rinse rice well and soak for several hours. Boil in 3 cups salted water until tender. Rinse.

1 to 1½ C chopped onion

1 to 2 C thinly sliced celery

3 slices bacon, cut in bits

½ green pepper, chopped (optional)

1 C sliced fresh mushrooms (optional)

2 beaten eggs

2 T soy sauce

1 can (6 oz.) shrimp (drained) or 1 C cooked fresh shrimp, or

1 C roast chicken or turkey, or 1 C fresh cooked crayfish

This is a flexible recipe, which needs no exact amount and invites your ingenuity.

Fry bacon, removing bits; also take out 2 T bacon fat to scramble eggs in separate pan. With fry pan at about 300°, sauté or stir-fry onions and celery in remaining bacon fat for about 3 minutes. Add peppers and mushrooms if used and continue to stir-fry about 2 minutes longer, but keep the vegetables crisp.

Meanwhile, scramble eggs in separate pan and cut them into small bits. Add eggs, bacon bits, cooked wild rice. Sprinkle and stir in soy sauce. Lightly stir mixture, heat but do not cook. Serve at once. Serves 4.

Wild Rice Stuffing

Use the basic wild rice recipe with ⅓ cup instead of ⅔ cup uncooked wild rice. And dissolve 4 chicken bouillon cubes in the 3 cups water instead of using plain water. Do not rinse.

⅓ C wild rice	1 medium onion diced
4 chicken bouillon cubes	½ lb. mushrooms (optional)
2 C dry bread crumbs	1½ C chopped celery
4 slices bacon	½ t sage
1 T butter	½ t oregano

salt and pepper to taste

Place wild rice in colander and run cold water through it until the water runs clear. Cook rice in 3 cups bouillon water 45 minutes or until tender. Do not rinse after cooking. Cut bacon into small pieces, fry with onions and celery until bacon is crisp. Combine rice and bread crumbs, add bacon mixture, melted butter, salt and pepper, sage and oregano. Makes enough to stuff two or three mallard ducks or a large goose.

Wild Rice and Mushroom Stuffing

¼ C chopped onion	4 C cooked wild rice
1 C sliced mushrooms	1 t salt
⅓ C butter or margarine	Few grains pepper

Brown onion and mushroom in butter or margarine, and mix with other ingredients. Makes enough stuffing for 8- to 10-pound goose. Make half recipe for wild duck.

FISH, FOWL, FROGS & TURTLES

Before you catch that fish...

To preserve the delicate flavor and to keep them from spoiling, most fish species should be cleaned and chilled as quickly as possible after the catch. The juices in the flesh of fish are much like those in good meat. If you wash your fillets, use cold water, but never overwater or flood the flesh. When possible, dry fillets with a clean cloth or paper towel instead of washing. Carry plastic bags for your cleaned fish. These chill easily and hold in natural flavor and juices.

Now that you have the fish here's how...

To scale fish: Wash whole fish in fairly warm water; then chill in cold water immediately. Drain off water and grasp fish by tail using gloves for the spiny ones. With a knife, scrape off the scales toward the head, being careful not to break or cut the skin.

To clean fish: With a sharp knife, using gloves and watching out for sharp spines, start to cut off head in back of the gills removing the two pectoral fins and ventral fins. Make a short slit down the belly to the vent, cut through the backbone and grasp the head, gently twisting and pulling off the head with the entrails still attached.

To skin fish: Omit scaling procedure and proceed to clean fish as above. Then slice off dorsal and anal fins. Cut the skin around the tail and finish slitting the skin down the back and belly. With pliers, start at the tail and pull off the skin in two sections. (For catfish, use a cloth in order to hang on to the slippery tail.)

To fillet fish: After the fish has been cleaned as above, use a sharp knife to cut along each side of the backbone. Working one side at a time, front end to tail, slice carefully down to and over the rib cage bones and the rest of the body. Small fish will yield two fillets; large fish need to be cut into uniform fillets for cooking as desired.

Oven Fried Fish

Dip about 1 pound fillets of bass or bluegill in 1 slightly beaten egg. Then roll fish in fine cracker or dry bread crumbs. Place in greased shallow baking pan, in a single layer. Sprinkle with paprika, salt and pepper (lemon pepper is good, too). Dot generously with butter or margarine. Bake at 375° for about ½ hour or until fish flakes easily when tested with a fork. Serve with lemon or tartar sauce.

NOTE: Unskinned whole trout or small whole bluegill or bass that have been scaled may also be cooked by this method.

Camper's Grilled Trout

Clean, rinse and dry fish. Brush with oil and sprinkle with seafood seasoning. Shape a shallow pan out of aluminum foil. Brush pan with oil or spray before putting in fish. Place over glowing coals and cook until fish flakes easily when tested with a fork. If the weather doesn't cooperate, place the fish under the broiler for 4 to 5 minutes. Serve with lemon wedge and a sprig of parsley.

Basic Fritter Batter

2 eggs	1 t baking powder
1 C milk	1 t salt
1 C all-purpose flour	2 t melted shortening

Put eggs in small mixing bowl and beat for one minute. Add milk, flour, baking powder, salt and shortening. Deep fat fry fish fillets, clams, or mussels for 2 to 3 minutes at 400°.

Catfish Balls

Cook as soon as possible after catching. Bake or steam catfish until tender enough to remove the meat from the bones. Flake meat. To every 2 cups catfish add 2 cups mashed potatoes, 1 egg, 1 teaspoon minced parsley, celery salt and pepper to taste. Shape in balls and fry in deep fat.

Cooking Hints for Clams or Mussels

Dip whole, cleaned clams or mussels in slightly beaten eggs, roll in cracker crumbs or flour. Fry rapidly in hot oil until brown on both sides, or deep fat fry until brown.

Mussel Patties

1 pint ground mussels or clams

¾ C cracker crumbs

2 or 3 beaten eggs

1 T melted butter

Dash or two seafood seasoning

Salt and pepper

½ C milk or clam juice

Combine mixture to make a consistency right to form patties and drop from spoon. Fry in hot fat about 375° until brown on both sides.

Clam Chowder

4-6 medium potatoes, diced	2 large cans milk
1 medium onion, diced	3 C water
4 strips bacon, crumbled	Pinch basil and thyme
1 C ground or minced clams	Parsley to garnish

Salt and pepper to taste

In a 4-quart pan fry bacon crisp. Crumble bacon and set aside. In about 3 T bacon fat sauté onions and potatoes until browned lightly. Add raw clams, cover with water. (You may want to pre-cook the clams.) Cook until potatoes and clams are tender. Cool, add milk, bacon and about 3 cups water. Heat slowly, but do not boil. Makes about eight 1-cup servings.

Clam Bake

Sauté a cup of celery, peppers and onions until lightly browned. Add ½ cup chopped toast or croutons, splash of dry vermouth, 2 cups ground or chopped clams or mussels and a whole egg. Add thyme or tabasco sauce. Put into empty shell or small individual casseroles. Pop into oven at 350° for about 20 minutes. Sprinkle on paprika as garnish.

Preparing and Cooking Frogs

First remove hind legs. Using a sharp knife, loosen the skin as you pull it down the leg and over the feet. Cut off feet and rinse well in cold water. Then pull out the long leg tendons. This prevents the legs from jumping around in the skillet! Soak in salt water for about an hour. Drain, pat dry with towels. Roll in flour; then dip in beaten egg; roll again in flour or cracker or bread crumbs. Fry in butter in a moderately hot fry pan. Brown for several minutes on each side and serve at once. Resembles chicken in taste and texture, and is absolutely delicious!

Steamed Crayfish

Wash about 5 lbs. of crayfish in clean water, place in heavily salted water for several minutes, then rinse again in fresh water. Heat a large pot of water to boiling. Add two chopped onions, several stalks chopped celery, 2 sliced lemons, 2 cloves garlic, several peppercorns, 3 or 4 bay leaves and ½ pound salt; then add the crayfish.

After crayfish have boiled five minutes, turn off heat, cover pot and soak 20 to 30 minutes. They should be ready to peel off shells and eat, hot or in your favorite recipe.

Roasted Wild Duck or Goose

After cleaning bird, soak in salt water overnight. Use 1 teaspoon salt to 1 quart of water. Remove from salt water, wipe dry. Season cavity with salt and pepper and stuff with Wild Rice Stuffing (see recipe, page 86), regular bread stuffing, whole onion, or apple. Skewer, rub skin with salt, pepper and shortening. Place in roaster with just enough water to cover the bottom. Cover and roast at 350° for 1½ to 2 hours, for a duck, or until tender. For a goose, roast for about 3 to 4 hours or until tender. Remove cover of roaster for final 20 minutes to allow the skin to brown.

Kotulas' Hints on Cleaning Turtles

First chop off the head. Then hang by the tail for about 2 hours to let the blood drain. Cut off carapace, skin, wash and cut in pieces suitable for one of the following methods of cooking.

Mrs. K's Fried Turtle

Flour pieces, season with salt and pepper. Brown in hot margarine, reduce heat, cover and cook until tender. Browned pieces may be put into a greased covered casserole and baked until tender. Serve with barbecue sauce.

Turtle Chowder

½ C diced turtle	2 C water
½ t salt	1 small onion
3 medium potatoes	1 medium carrot
1 large tomato fresh or cooked	pinch sweet basil
2 slices crisp bacon bits	salt and pepper to taste

Cook turtle meat in salted water until tender. Add diced potatoes, carrots, onion and tomato. Cook 30 minutes or until vegetables are tender. Add bacon and seasonings. More water or milk may be added to make mixture soupy.

Turtle and Wild Rice Delight

½ C wild rice	¼ t oregano
½ C onions, chopped	⅛ t black pepper
½ C celery, chopped	½ t salt
¼ C slivered almonds	1 T butter

2½ C water
¾ pound fresh or frozen turtle or
1½ pounds turtle with bones

Run cold water through rice in a sieve until water runs clear. Place rice and other ingredients in crock pot. Cook about 5 hours or until turtle is tender. Remove meat from bones, chop, and stir back into rice mixture. Serve with dash of soy sauce or curry if desired. About 4 servings. (NOTE: The raw rice and the rest of ingredients may be baked in a covered casserole at 350° for about 2 hours or until rice and turtle are tender.)

GLOSSARY

alternate: growing in any arrangement along a stem that is neither opposite nor whorled.

anal: pertaining to or situated near the anus.

annual: a plant that grows, blooms or flowers, goes to seed, and dies within a year.

axil: the upper angle between the stem or branch and the leaf.

cambium: a delicate layer of tissue between the inner bark and the wood, which produces new plant cells, creating the annual rings.

cilia: numerous microscopic, whiplike hairs that flutter rapidly to move a material.

compound leaf: composed of a number of leaflets on a common stalk.

deciduous: applied to plants that loose their leaves in the autumn of the year.

dorsal: refers to the back or upper side of an animal's body.

elliptical: egg-shaped, or more long than round.

herbaceous: plants that are not woody.

leaflets: in a compound leaf, one of the separate divisions of the leaf.

lobed: having divisions extending less than halfway to the middle of the base of a leaf.

node: the joint of stem and leaf.

opposite: situated on diametrically opposed sides of a stem, as when there are two leaves on one node.

pectoral: pertaining to the breast or chest area, as in a fin on the side of a fish.

perennial: having a life cycle of more than two years.

pistils: the part of the plant that produces seeds.

rootstalks: underground rootlike stems that can send up shoots.

species: an interfertile group of organisms bearing common characters which distinguish them from other groups.

sphagnum: a genus of soft moss found chiefly on the surface of bogs.

spikelet: a small, elongated cluster of flowers in grasses.

stamen: the organ which carries pollen in a flowering plant.

strobile: the somewhat conical multiple fruit of various trees.

ventral: refers to the belly or lower side of an animal's body.

whorled: arranged in a circular array around a single node or joint on a stem.

SELECTED READING LIST

For further pond life information, you will find the following books helpful.

Abrams, Leroy, *Illustrated Flora of the Pacific States*, 4 Vols., Stanford University Press, Stanford, California, 1960.

Amos, William H., *The Life of the Pond*, McGraw-Hill, Inc., New York, NY, 1967.

Berglund, Berndt and Clare E. Bolsby, *The Edible Wild*, Charles Scribner's Sons, New York, NY, 1971.

Clark, Lewis, J., *Wild Flowers of Marsh and Waterway in the Pacific Northwest*, Gray's Publ. Limited, Sidney, B. C., Canada, 1974.

Furlong, Marjorie and Virginia Pill, *Wild Edible Fruits and Berries*, Naturegraph Publishers, Happy Camp, CA, 1974.

Hotchkiss, Neil, *Common Marsh, Underwater and Floating-leaved Plants of the United States and Canada*, Dover Publications, Inc., New York, NY, 1972.

Kirk, Donald R., *Wild Edible Plants of Western North America*, Naturegraph Publishers, Happy Camp, CA, 1970, 1975.

Reid, George K., *Pond Life, A Guide to Common Plants and Animals of North American Ponds and Lakes*, Golden Press, New York, NY, 1967.

Rickett, Theresa C., *Wild Flowers of Missouri*, University of Missouri Press, Columbia, Missouri, 1954.

Scully, Virginia, *A Treasury of American Indian Herbs*, Crown Publishers, Inc., New York, NY, 1970.

Turner, Nancy J., *Food Plants of British Columbia Indians*, Part 1, Coastal Peoples, British Columbia Provincial Museum, Victoria, B. C., Canada, 1975.

Ursin, Michael J., *Life in and Around Freshwater Wetlands, A guide to plants and animals in wetlands east of the Mississippi*, Thomas Y. Crowell Co., New York, NY, 1975.

Weldon, L. W., R. D. Blackburn, and D. S. Harrison, *Common Aquatic Weeds*, Dover Publications, Inc., New York, NY, 1973.

Zim, Herbert S. et al., *The Rocky Mountains*, Golden Press, New York, NY, 1964.

Zim, Herbert S. and Hobart M. Smith, *Reptiles and Amphibians*, Golden Press, New York, NY, 1953.

INDEX

(Page numbers in italics refer to recipe suggestions.)

Mint, 18-19, *76, 79, 80*
Mountain Labrador Tea, 45
Mussels, 58-59, 71, *89*

Nasturtium officinale, 31-32
Nettles, 20-21, *84*
Nuphar spp., 16-17
Nymphaea odorata, 15-16
Phragmites communis, 24
Pondweed, 22-23
Populus trichocarpa, 39
Potamogeton natans, 22-23

PROPERTY OF SCHMIDT CENTER

Rana spp., 64-66
Reed Grass, 24, 26, *83*
Ribes lacustre, 43
Rosa spp., 50-51
Rubus spectabilis, 46
Rushes, 25, 26, *79, 83*

Sagittaria latifolia, 29-30
Salix spp., 52
Salmo spp., 69-71
Salmonberry, 46, *76, 78*
Salvelinus fontinalis, 70
Sedges, 26, *79, 83, 84*
Skunk Cabbage, 27-28
Sparganium spp., 11-12
Squashberry, 47-48, *79*
Swamp Laurel, 41, 45

Trionyx muticus, 72-74
Trout, 69-71, *87, 88*
Turtles, 60, *72-74, 91*
Twinberry, 49, *76, 78*
Typha spp., 13-14

Urtica dioica, 20-21

Vaccinium occidentale, 37-38
Vaccinium Oxycoccus var. intermedium, 41-42
Viburnum edule, 47-48

Wapato, 29-30, *81, 83*
Watercress, 31-32, *82*
Wild Rice, 33-34, *85, 86*
Wild Rose, 50-51, *80, 81*
Willow, 52

Zizania aquatica, 33-34

95

RELATED BOOKS FROM NATUREGRAPH

WILD EDIBLE FRUITS & BERRIES, by Marjorie Furlong and Virginia Pill. A full-color photograph and detailed description accompany each of the 42 fruits and berries described in this book. Delicious recipes add to the reader's fun and good eating. The book locates species primarily in the Northwest, and encourages conservation principles. 64 pages.

WILD EDIBLE PLANTS OF WESTERN NORTH AMERICA—Color Edition, by Donald Kirk. This popular book covers nearly 2000 species of wild edibles from western Canada to northern Mexico. 64 color plates and over 400 drawings provide detailed identification. Includes methods of preparation and use. 343 pages.

KNOW YOUR POISONOUS PLANTS, by Wilma James. Here are descriptions and identifying illustrations of 154 commonly cultivated or naturally growing plants. The author offers methods of treatment and prevention of poisoning. A must for hikers and families. 100 pages.

NATURAL REMEDIES FOR BETTER HEALTH, by Dr. Ingrid Sherman. This standard title on how to use natural foods, physical, mental and spiritual exercises, and other wholesome ways to attain balanced living is in its tenth printing. It includes many old household recipes which are easy and inexpensive, and lists uses of plants. 128 pages.

COUNTRY LAND—And Its Uses, by Howard Orem and Suzen. Chock-full of information for living in harmony with nature, this book is in four sections: Land Selection, Land Development, Water Development, and Organic Gardening. Diagrams show how to construct buildings, water tanks, windmills, solar heating systems, etc. 310 pages.

PROPAGATE YOUR OWN PLANTS, by Wilma James. This is a fully-illustrated guide to selecting, propagating, and caring for indoor and outdoor plants—over 700 in all. Emphasizing use of available vegetation, the author explains modern methods for cuttings, runners, division, layering, etc. 149 pages.

AMERICAN WILDLIFE REGION SERIES. These compact guide books for the hiker describe the flora and fauna as well as other important natural history facts of major regions: The California Wildlife Region; The Pacific Coastal Wildlife Region; The Sierra Nevadan Wildlife Region; The California Chaparral—An Elfin Forest; Wildlife and Plants of the Cascades; Wildlife of the Intermountain West; Wildlife of the Northern Rocky Mountains; Wildlife and Plants of the Southern Rocky Mountains. More volumes to come.

Ask for these titles at your nearest bookstore, or write to Naturegraph Books, Happy Camp, CA 96039, for a free catalog.